ALOHA COOKING
Paul Freeman

ALOHA COOKING

Paul Freeman

ALOHA COOKING

Paul Freeman

PUBLISHED *by* PARABLES
Earthly Stories with a Heavenly Meaning

ALOHA COOKING
Paul Freeman

ALOHA COOKING
Paul Freeman

Published By Parables
May, 2022

Printed in the United States of America

Readers should be aware that Internet Web sites offered as citations and/or sources for further information may have been changed or disappeared between the time this was written and the time it is read.

ALOHA COOKING

Paul Freeman

PUBLISHED by PARABLES
Earthly Stories with a Heavenly Meaning

ALOHA COOKING
Paul Freeman

ALOHA COOKING
Paul Freeman

ALOHA COOKING

Paul Freeman

ALOHA COOKING
Paul Freeman

INTRODUCTION

Aloha from the Hawaiian Islands, to your Pu'uwai from ours, Pu'uwai meaning Heart. What are your thoughts of Hawaii's Foods? Well whatever your answer is to that question isn't wrong or far off. Because the simple fact is that the many foods of Hawaii are a melting pot of luscious, flavory stews. It's mouthwatering, satisfying seasonings and spices will take you away like the strong ocean tides pulling you out to the sea. Hawaii's foods don't just consist of our old traditional Hawaiian cuisine. Our local Hawaiian foods are filled with the many different ethnicities and cultures that's been melted together forming one big Ohana, Ohana meaning Family.

From this book of loving to cook you will come to find that there is joy and happiness in what we eat and you will also find that joy and happiness are in the cooking and the response from others.

In Hawaii, the palm trees sway in the beautiful warm weather, where you can feel the aloha spirit. Try to envision the vast ocean surrounding our islands, the white caps of the endless waves, as we surf them or just bathing in the nice warm sun-rays, catching a golden tan. Imagine the hidden waterfalls you could find as you hike the many trails. Breathtaking as these Hawaiian Islands are, my hope is that you will be captivated and experience a little of the islands in what you'll learn from this book.

This could shock you if you haven't experienced shopping in a supermarket such as you would find in Hawaii. I can still remember this certain supermarket, its emporium shelves of foods and treats, its perfect introductions of Hawaii's foods with the many isles of fruits, vegetables, cultural canned and packaged goods which cannot be compared to the mainland supermarkets. It all goes beyond just that, as you'll soon know, in addition from what the mainland has, Hawaii's supermarkets provide complete sections of vast cultural foods. From Pilipino goods to make the many homemade meals. Such as pork adobo, lumpia, halo halo, and many more. There are also rows of Japanese foods, ranging from fresh treat to canned delights and even dehydrated snacks of deliciousness. Followed by a section of Korean foods which I've grown to love through my life growing up on these Hawaiian Islands of Aloha.

I still remember from my times at my childhood friend's grandma's house, how she would make her Korean Kim Chee from scratch. She used these large empty Best Foods Mayonnaise jars and added all her assorted spices with cabbage, then letting it ferment over a long period of time. These fermented vegetables are used as a side dish for meals or a tasty treat to snack on anytime of the day.

Beyond the Korean aisle is a Chinese section of deliciousness with an ancient Chinese secret. Don't tell anyone that I told you about their secret ingredient called Five Spice. L.O.L. Jokes on you...then in the grand center of the supermarket which contains

ALOHA COOKING
Paul Freeman

mainly Polynesian edibles such as taro, mangos, coconuts, and papaya – either fresh or dehydrated, to assorted delicacy treats and so much more. As you walk through the store, the aroma of the wide variety of fresh products fills the air. There are even a few aisles of Puerto Rican, Portuguese, and Mexican foods imported from various countries around the world. This supermarket that I still remember always comes to mind whenever anyone speaks about Hawaiian cooking. A Hawaiian home cooked meal takes advantage of the many different selections of culture, great traditional styles, and tastes of the many different countries that make up its population. One would have to visit and experience the fullness of our Hawaiian island style of Aloha not just cooking but also our heartfelt Aloha that we islanders share with each other as well as all those that come to Hawaii. Yet the "Aloha of Cooking" (The Love of Cooking!) is written so that you will have a better understanding of what I have experienced and am attempting to share with you. You'll come to know that even if you go to a luau, party or a pot-luck, you could find a Korean dish, a Japanese dish, a Puerto Rican dish, or any of the many different cultures named earlier. The island style, aloha of cooking, finds its way to the table to be feasted upon and filling our bellies in a way that also entertains. A twist here and there in the ways we islanders often prepare and cook the countless meals and treats, offers a delightful variety for endless ways to enjoy. This book is strong and colorfully customized to reach a wide audience. Just as the island is a blend of many different cultures, so is the island's cooking a mix of its many different cuisines. One must balance for their self the culinary arts from this book and achieve their passion for "the love of cooking. "ALOHA COOKING"

ALOHA COOKING
Paul Freeman

ALOHA COOKING

Paul Freeman

Preface

Hawaii's cooking is a delicious adventure in eating as well as a warm heartfelt experience. It embraces foods from all walks of people that have made Hawaii their home. The Hawaiian, Polyanions, Chinese, Japanese, Filipinos, Korean, Porto Ricans, Portuguese, Mexican, and all American. "LOCAL Hawaiian cooking" has become a way of life on the islands, for it opens one's mind. More importantly, it opens up your pallet to different tastes, cooking techique, to a variety of cultures, and the people themselves. I hope this book and your experiences with it will enrich your life as you prepare your next feast, or as we call them, luau's. On a personal level my passion for LOCAL Hawaiian cooking started for so many different and meaning full seasonings and spices.

A great friend of mine, "The William S. Graham", once asked me to write why I love to cook. And what first came to mind was the flood of loving, thoughtful memories of being in the kitchen. Cooking meals with my dear, loving mom and how we would cook an ohana meal, a "family meal". So here I am hoping to share my passion with all of you who love cooking and those who would like to learn.

So let's put on them cooking aprons, and heat up them stoves and grills. We are going on a cooking expedition like you've never gone on before. With me as

ALOHA COOKING
Paul Freeman

your chef and cooking guide, I will not just show you the many joys and happiness of cooking, I am going to open up your mana's and Pu'uwai (your mind and heart), as I teach you the meaning of "Aloha Cooking. I can go on telling you why I love to cook, but the question at hand is, why should we love to cook? Because it's a healthy and beneficial life skill that we all ought to learn whether it's for a luau for our loved ones, the simplest snack bites we might crave throughout the day, or to satisfy our cravings for some late night munchies.

Some people have cooking instilled into them by cultural tradition. Perhaps this is the reason why we love to cook. Of course that's just one perspective. There are many chefs in the world who cook for a living, but aren't passionate about their craft. For some, it's just a job that pays the bills. So my question to you is, how passionate are you for cooking, are you excited to learn new things? I for one love cooking with a passion for so many different reasons. It brings joy and happiness to me. I am still moved by the deep emotions of laughter shared in the kitchen cooking with my grandma and mom.

It goes beyond just my Hawaiian island traditions, nationality and ethnicity. I love to see the overwhelming joy and happiness in peoples' expressions that food brings to them as they bite into the tastiness of foods and treats I've prepared. By having that love for cooking, it gives me a sense of such a peaceful and heartfelt feeling. So as you take this journey with me to love the art of cooking, remember to enjoy yourselves. Included within are familiar recipes with some unique twists. I encourage you to experiment

ALOHA COOKING
Paul Freeman

and tweak them to your own liking. Your love and respect for food is the very beginning to these lessons. For without these qualities we wouldn't get very far. You must be attentive to the most minor details and be patient. Some steps in preparing and cooking these meals takes its necessary time.

I'm honored that you are collaborating with me. You are always most welcome to add your own twist of flavors to these dishes, treats, and beverages. It's what will make your dish that much more special to love. Bringing food to life is a very eloquent art. It can take you further than you could imagine with just a splash of this, a pinch of that, and a sprinkle of love, and you'll have yourself the tastiest meals and treats.

My favorite traditional Hawaiian dishes include Kalua pig, Lomi Lomi Salmon, Poi, and even some Haupia; let me stop myself there because I could go on forever naming them all. I've said enough, and we need to get a move on with me sharing the Aloha of Cooking with you all.

Yet before we begin, a special mahalo, meaning "thank you", to my bra dahs and friends, to William S. Graham and Sean Marshall, for encouraging me to step out of my realm of loving to cook into writing a book about it, for their caring support in mentoring me, for brotherly, heartfelt friendship that I will cherish for the rest of my life. You've opened my eyes to see the world beyond what I've known until now, To me words aren't enough to express my deepest gratitude to the both of you. Just know that that the both of you are a part of my Ohana "FAMILY".

ALOHA COOKING
Paul Freeman

Mahalo My Bra dahs.

ALOHA COOKING
Paul Freeman

A Brief History of Hawaii

When it comes to Hawaii's local foods, you'll first have to understand its history such as when the Polynesians who were the first arrived to these islands that we call the Hawaiian Islands. The kanaka maoli, the native Hawaiians of old, taught us how to live off the Ina, which is the "land", and the vast ocean that surrounds us with its richness of foods. Manageable systems that supply them and us to this very day.

The very meaning of Aloha, that cultivated unconditional Love and compassion for the Ina (land) and po'e (the people) continue to resonate with the people. Even though the old rulers of the kanaka maoli are no longer around, their mana is still felt. Yes, their spirit is felt and seen in so many ways: the poke or the package poi that sits on the grocery store shelves the welcoming feeling at the family or friend's luau and in celebrations we eat of the old traditional foods like the kalua pig, laulau, poke, poi, haupia and many other old traditional foods its survival endures throughout the past several centuries.

I am honored to speak of such a testament of my people and being a kama'aina, a child of the land, native born. Alongside the arrival of the Brits and other Europeans came Captain James Cook to the Hawaiian Islands in 1778. The Hawaiians were not as advance as the Europeans in their daily life which resulted in a culture clash. Living in harmony on the islands has never been the same since.

Yes, we still have peace, yet that true paradise garden of Eden sense of living is no longer there. Take it from me, who was been born and raised in Hawaii, on the beautiful island of Oahu... the most modernized of our islands. From Kamehameha The Great, who had united all of Hawaii's people, to the overthrow of Hawaii's royal monarchy starting with king Kalakaua in 1887 and five years later fully overthrowing Hawaii's government by imprisoning queen Liliuokalani. The lawless act of the United States against Hawaii and its people which annexed the islands in 1898, making us an official American territory. Years later the Hawaiian islands became the 50th state in 1959.

The vast changes since has been an enormous leap its imports and exports of goods has large amounts of economic movement had and currently still does impact Hawaii's people and its islands.

Its toll from long ago until now has been as follows generations ago when disease introduced by the Europeans was lethal. European colonization extracted a heavy toll with the subjugation of our people, the introduction of diseases, and the widespread theft of our resources. It is estimated that the population of Hawaii was brutally reduced from 800,000 to only 150,000.

Yet we have expanded back into the millions with the help of many other ethnicities, creating a culture so heavenly divine, it's a melting pot of aloha "love". Our immigrant groups range from Pilipino, Chinese, Japanese, Korean, Portuguese, Puerto Rican, and even the many other different pacific islanders such as Samoans, Tahitians, Fijians, Marians, Tongans, etc.

ALOHA COOKING
Paul Freeman

Our identity has grown and we have flourished, cultivating a living breathing culture of aloha. Yet it took a lot of time. Back then, during the segregation of the ethnic groups, was not an easy. Yet, gradually through it all, our history has brought our foods and language together to a common ground that we continue to build on to this very day.

An expression of the shaking of a hand, saying shaka, is a communication and acknowledgement between us. When it comes down to Hawaii's history what will you see? The living breathing food culture with its many differences that has brought us into harmony? Or its shared pigeon language? Its mana of the many people? Mana meaning spirit of aloha.

So as you read through this cookbook, and cook yourself a meal or treat, remember the roots of its origin. Not its distant origin but the origin of today in Hawaii Na.

ALOHA COOKING
Paul Freeman

ALOHA COOKING

Paul Freeman

BEVERAGES.

So what's a meal without a nice stiff drink? Still a meal; you really don't need a drink with every meal. Yet at times it's a great complement to some meals. Even a nice cold beer goes well with so many dishes. I'm no expert in that department, yet I do know that to some people, a little glass of wine enriches one's pallet, as well as cleanses it the way lemon water refreshes the taste buds, allowing a more favorable experience to open up for another flavorful taste. So here are a few drinks that you may try at your next party or couple's candlelight dinner. Do remember that not all drinks go with every meal.

MAI TAI

This drink is very well known for its tropical sweet pineapple citrus taste, as well as its long garnish stalk of pineapple that protrudes out of the glass.

<u>Ingredients</u>

2 oz. light rum	½ oz. orange curacao
2 oz. orange juice	2 oz. lemon juice
4 oz. pineapple juice	2 oz. dark rum

<u>Instructions</u>

Step 1: Combined and mix all ingredient except the dark rum. Mix well and pour over crushed ice in a tall glass.

Step 2: Then float the dark rum on top of glass drink.

Step 3: Garnish drink with a long stalk of fresh pineapple and a gardenia or orchid.

Makes two drinks.

SWEET PICKLED MANGO PALOMAS

Ingredients

1 cup tequila reposado
2 12 oz. can grapefruit
juice
2 lemon halves

Hawaiian salt for garnish

1 large package wet or dry
sweet pickle mango

Instructions

Step 1: Combine in a jar tequila and sweet pickled mango. Let these ingredients marinate together in the fridge over night or at least for one hour.

Step 2: Take four Collin glass and wet its rim, then dip the rim of the glass into Hawaiian salt. Fill glasses ¾ full with ice.

Step 3: Then evenly divide tequila mango mixture in glass. Top glass with four to six ounces of the grapefruit soda.

Step 4: Squeeze in lemon halves, give it a little stir, and there you go, a sweet pickled mango palomas for your delight.

Who says you can't have your cake and ice cream at the same time? Not in this adventure, with me as your guide through the love of cooking. Remember that you can put your own twist to your creating of this drink, or any other recipe in this book. For instance, dip the rim of glass in tabasco sauce instead of water and salt the rim, or splash the rim with some chili pepper water. These are just a couple ways to spice up your drink.

NOTES: This is just a little something I put together to have you open up your minds to trying different things. So what are your thoughts on this twist of a drink that you may have had in its original form? I myself love sweet pickled mango, and mixing it into a palomas blends mildly together just right. So take one of your own favorite drinks and your choice of fruit or liquor, fusing them together to create a master piece of your very own unique and vibrant blend.

ALOHA COOKING
Paul Freeman

NO-MO PAIN
Ingredients
1 1/2 oz. okolehao = rum
thin slice lemon
½ oz. dry sherry

green chartreus
2 dash of tabasco
cube of sugar

Instructions
Step 1: Combine the first three ingredients and pour mixture over shaved ice in an old fashion glass.
Step 2: Then garnish with lemon slice and cube of sugar, add green chartreuse over the cube of sugar, then light the drink on fire. Please be very careful when preforming this process,
WE don't want you to light yourself on fire. This is a cook book, not a Smokey the Bear commercial, "Only you can prevent forest fire." We don't want more pain, were looking for no-mo pain. So let's say you're having a bad day, or things aren't going the way you planned them to go (Murphy's Law right, when anything can go wrong, they'll go wrong?). Something like that so don't quote me on that. But what you can take to the bank is that the beverage "No-Mo Pain" will ease your daily anguish away.

ALOHA

Ingredients

3 oz. *okolehao* = *rum*	1 oz. lemon Juice
1 oz. cherry liqueur	1 dash Grenadine

Instructions

Step 1: Shake the four ingredients with crushed ice.

Step 2: Strain mixture into a chilled champagne glass and garnish with Vanda orchid.

Wasn't that simple? Of course it was, that's just a little something to put your mind at ease. You can put any twist you like to it, such as adding mint or a little fresh fruit, as well as a splash of soda water. Now that you got your first taste of what's to come, what are some of your thoughts? I would like to share with you a whole lot more. Yet to not bore you all. I plan on keeping things in a decent amount of measures. I just don't want to overwhelm you with too much, at one time. Do understand that I don't want to lose you all with over piling your plates too high so that you get stuffed with all its goodness. Don't you agree?

So do look forward to the second edition of ALOHA COOKING with me Sahn Lorenzo Freeman. I'm sure to keep your appetite Satisfied. ALOHA....

PUPUS

PUPU'S This is the Hawaii's way of saying HORS D'OEUVRES, or finger foods. Now there is heavy PUPUS LUAU'S that will blow your mind away. You would think that all the foods are main dishes or main courses at some of the luaus or parties that we host in Hawaii. So come and enjoy with us the many PUPU'S, just don't overdo yourself when it comes to these tasty delights. Now come with me on the wonderful road of PUPU LAND.

HAWAIIAIN PUPU CHICKEN WINGS

This stick, crunchy, intensely garlicky flavorful chicken wings come from a recipe that I was taught when I was growing up in Hawaii. The double fry is the best if you have that time and patience with going that extra mile. Yet that is for another time my friends, I am just wanting you all to come custom to what I'm teaching

Ingredients

1 tablespoon sesame seed oil

2 tablespoon unseasoned rice wine vinegar

2 tablespoon toasted sesame seeds

3 garlic cloves finely minced

6 green onion finely chopped and save 1/3 for garnish at the end

1 ½ teaspoon crushed red pepper flake

2 tablespoon concentrated pineapple juice

2 pound mini chicken wing, tips remove

¾ cup soy sauce

ALOHA COOKING
Paul Freeman

1/3 cup sugar
½ of a lemon
1 cup potato starch or all-purpose flour
2-3 cups coconut oil or any other high smoke-point oil

Instructions
Step 1: Put the first 10 ingredients in a sauce pan and briefly bring to a boil.
 Step 2: Then pat chicken and coat with potato starch thoroughly shaking off excess starch or flour.
 Step 3: Per heat in Wok or Dutch oven the 2-3 Cups of coconut oil or any high smoke point oil heat at 350*F.
 Step 4: Gently lower coated chicken wings in 5-6 at a time don't over crowd pan. Allow wings to cook to a nice brown turn wing and repeat to a nice brown.12 to 15 mins for each batch. Remove chicken wings and place in a bowl to rest 3-5 mins. then into sauce pan.
 Step 5: Take Chicken wings from the sauce pan allowing remaining sauce to drip off. place wing onto a serving plate and garnish with green onion.

SPAM MOSOBI

Ingredients

2 12 oz. can spam
½ cup sugar
½ cup soy sauce
8 cups cooked rice

4 tablespoons Mirin
1 large pack Sushi nori sheet
4 teaspoons Furikake

Instructions

Step 1: Slice spam into 6 pieces per each can of spam. Fry the spam for 4-5 mins or until a nice browning outside, remove and set aside in a clean pan. Add the soy sauce, sugar and mirin, stir together and bring to a boil. Then reduce heat to low return spam to sauce pan coat, cook until a sticky glaze forms. Remove off heat let it set until ready to use.

Step 2: Toast the nori sheets 15-20 seconds over a gas stove or a hot oven for 1-2 minutes. Prepare a bowl of warm water. If you have a Musubi mold, then fill the mold with a nice ¾ inch high and if you don't have a mold. Then use a flat bottom topper wear container press down rice ¾ inch high and use the empty spam lid

Step 3: Place cut strips of Nori sheet wraps to the size of spam and rice On a clean flat surface place rice top with Furikake then the glaze spam with a little glaze sauce. Dab the nori edge with warm water to seal your wrapped musubi continue until all musubi is wrapped. Serve right away, best eaten immediately

NOTES: Mosobi is something that can be enjoyed in a variety of different ways. You could choose not to use spam or any meat to make a mosobi. The original mosobi just has a red dyed soy bean in the middle instead of spam. You could use fresh vegetables in your mosobi, but not with this recipe. It's called spam mosobi for that very reason – it has SPAM! So please enjoy this finger food that we islanders have loved for its simple tastiness.

CRUSTED AHI SASHIMI

Ingredients
1 large Ahi filet, tuna.
1/3 cup Furikake
1/3 cup crushed Wonton chips

1 1/2 tablespoon sesame seed

Instructions
Step 1: Crush Wonton chips and mix it with the sesame seeds and Furikake.
Step 2: Pat Ahi dry and season ahi with salt and pepper.
Step 3: Coat Ahi with the crushed mixture of sesame, Furikake, and Wonton.
Step 4: Pre-heat frying pan on medium high, just sear for about 20-30 seconds on each side, let cool. Then cut sashimi style using a very sharp knife. Plate and serve.
Notes: You may choose from the many varieties of sauce that this book has for you, or use a sauce that you might like to put to the test. Who knows, you might hit a home run with your inner Babe Ruth. Yet here's a honey mustard sauce that may interest you. Give it a try.
For this quick and easy sauce add ingredients below.

Ingredients
2 tablespoon honey
1/4 cup soy sauce
1/3 cup mustard

1 teaspoon Tabasco sauce
¼ wedge of a lemon squeezed

Mix well, to a nice smooth consistence, Dip and enjoy

CRISPY GAU GEE

Ingredients

3 pound ground pork	1 tablespoon oyster sauce
24 oz. pk. Wonton skin	1/3 cup sliced scallions
2 eggs +2 Egg whites	1½ soy sauce
10 cloves garlic mince	1 ½ tablespoon fish sauce
3 teaspoons cornstarch	Neutral oil for frying
¾ pound peel Lg shrimp finely mince	
4 tablespoons mince fresh ginger	

Instructions

Step 1: Mix in large bowl the pork, shrimp, garlic, ginger, egg whites, scallion, soy sauce, fish sauce, white pepper, and slur in cornstarch with 1 cup water. Then mix very well. Test the filling by taking a pinch of it and microwaving it adjust seasoning to your taste.

Step 2: Beat the 2 eggs in a small bowl.

Step 3: Place a tablespoon of filling into each Wonton skin. Dip finger in the bowl of beaten eggs, rub finger with beaten eggs on the edge of Wonton skin. Pinch edges to seal in filling in Wonton skin wraps. Repeat until filling is gone.

Step 4: Prepare wire rack or sheet pan with paper towel. Fill in a drop pot or Dutch oven 2 inches of oil, heat oil to 350*F use a thermometer must maintain temp.

Step 5: Don't over crowd pot let room for Wonton to move around. Cook until a nice golden brown. Place finish fried Wonton on wire rack or baking sheet let cool then serve with desired sauce.

ALOHA COOKING

Paul Freeman

NOTES: Sauces – sweet and sour sauce, soy sauce with mustard, siracha sauce, and the many other dips and sauces of your choice.

I remember many times going to a Chinese restaurant as a kid and having this wonderful treat. And what a treat it was, one that I remember to this very day. I just want you to know that it's not what you can do for the food that maters, what's more important is what the food does for you. I know that foods make me happy, it makes me smile, and it makes me feel really refreshing, to the point that I will share my last bite of food just so that another person can enjoy the very warm feeling that it brings me.

HAWAIIAIN SEA ANEMONES

<u>Ingredients</u>

2 teaspoon Sherry

4 cups Vegetable oil

7 waterchestnuts chopped

1 pound raw shrimp finely chopped

4 tablespoon scallion finely chopped

10 watercress finely chopped

2 tablespoons cornstarch

½ cup oriental vermicelli

2 tablespoon kosher salt

<u>Instructions</u>

Step 1: Combined all ingredients except vegetable oil. Coarsely mix them and scoop into round meatball shapes.

Step 2: Roll ball into cut vermicelli (bean thread) pressing lightly until covered.

Step 3: Deep fry these shrimp balls in hot oil. The vermicelli will puff up, turn white and crispy when cooked. Plate them and serve as finger foods.

ALOHA COOKING
Paul Freeman

COCONUT SHIRMP

Ingredients

1 ½ tablespoon oil

2 large egg whites

2 cloves garlic minced

2 pound fresh shrimp large

1 ½ teaspoon ginger finely minced

1 teaspoon kosher salt or to taste

1 ½ cups coconut shreds

1 cup flour and

2 teaspoons scallion copped

Instructions

Step 1: Clean shrimp cut in half down the back.

Step 2: Combine the garlic, ginger, coconut shreds, mix very well.

Step 3: Add to eggs, flour and beer/soda water, mixing it into a frying batter.

Step 4: Heat a drop pot or Dutch oven with 2 inches of oil. Use a thermometer to maintain temp.

Step 5: Dip shrimps in batter letting excess batter drip off. Place in pot don't over crowd pot. Cook until a golden brown, remove and let it rest on an air rack, then serve them up with any desired dips or sauce.

Notes: Enjoying this loving tasteful delights with family and friends. You'll come to mix your very own twist of wonders together, just remember its what's fitting to you as the cook, even when it comes to the desired taste or texture of your foods.

ALOHA COOKING
Paul Freeman

SALADS

MACORONI SALAD

Ingredients
12 oz. macaroni cooked
kosher salt
5 boiled eggs chopped
1 tablespoon garlic salt
1 stalk celery diced
2 ½ cups mayonnaise
1 small carrot grated
1/3 teaspoon paprika
1 teaspoon ground black pepper

Instructions
Step 1: Cook macaroni in a pot of salted water on high heat bring it to a boil cook until macaroni is tender. Rinse under cold water to cool the macaroni, then drain and refrigerate for 1 hour.
Step 2: In a large bowl mix in the chopped eggs, celery, carrots, mayonnaise, garlic salt, and ground black pepper.
Step 3: Fold in the chilled macaroni season to taste and garnish with paprika. Refrigerate until ready to serve.

HAWAIIAIN COLESLAW

Ingredients

1 cup pineapple diced

½ cup carrots grated

1 tablespoon olive oil

2 green onion sliced

1 ½ tablespoon honey

2 teaspoons sesame oil

1 small lemon for its juice

kosher salt

1 teaspoon black sesame seeds

2 cups green cabbage shredder

1 cup red cabbage shredded and pickled

3 tablespoons rice wine vinegar

1 tablespoon fresh ginger grated

Instructions

Step 1: Combine cabbages, pineapples, carrots, and green onion in a large bowl toss and set aside.

Step 2: Add olive oil, vinegar, honey, sesame oil, lemon juice, and ginger. Mix them very well, then pour mixture

over toss cabbages, toss again and coat cabbages
thoroughly. Season with salt to taste.
Step 3: Cover and refrigerate for 1 hour before serving,
garnish with black sesame seeds

POTATO SALAD

<u>Ingredients</u>
1/2teaspoon paprika
1 stalk celery diced
1/3 cup onion diced
2 cups mayonnaise
1 tablespoon mustard
kosher salt
½ tablespoon garlic salt
3 boiled eggs peeled and chopped
¼ cup chopped fresh parsley, cilantro
2 ½ pounds russet potatoes peeled and cut into ½ inch cubes
½ teaspoon ground black pepper

<u>Instructions</u>
Step 1: Heat large pot water with salt and add potatoes bring it to a boil. Then to a simmer cook until nice and tender. Drain and let cool then chill for 30 mins.
Step 2: In a large bowl mix in chopped eggs, mayonnaise, mustard, onion, garlic salt, ground black pepper and celery.
Step 3: Then fold in chilled potatoes and fresh herbs season to taste and garnish with paprika refrigerate until ready to serve.

ISLAND COLE SLAW

<u>Ingredients</u>
1/2 cup rice wine vinegar
2 tablespoons lime juice
¾ teaspoon kosher salt
1 red chili pepper diced
2 tablespoons sugar
1/3cup mayonnaise
½ cup pineapple diced
2 teaspoons sesame oil
1 tablespoon honey
¼ cup sour cream soften
1 med carrot, peeled shredded
1 cup thinly cut red cabbage 3 oz
1 teaspoon fresh ginger minced
2 cups thinly cut green cabbage 7 oz.

<u>Instructions</u>
Step 1: In large bowl add cabbages, carrots, pineapple, and chili pepper, tossing them together very well.
Step 2: Add sugar and vinegar whisk until sugar dissolves, then add ginger, sesame oil, sour cream mayonnaise, lemon juice, and honey whisk very well then combined mixture to the cabbage and toss coating cabbage evenly seasoning with salt and pepper.
Step 3: Cover and refrigerate for at least 30 minutes before serving.

EGG SALAD

<u>Ingredients</u>
kosher salt
1 teaspoon garlic salt
1/3 cup onion diced
1 stalk celery diced
½ teaspoon paprika
1 cup mayonnaise
2 eggs boiled and peeled
½ teaspoon ground black pepper
5 oz. black pitted olives sliced in half

<u>Instructions</u>
Step 1: In large bowl break up the 12 eggs, then add onions and celery.
Step 2: Add in mayonnaise, garlic salt, and ground black pepper to large bowl of eggs and fold them together well. Season with salt to taste.
Step 3: Garnish with black pitted olives and paprika, cover and refrigerate for 1 hour before serving.
NOTES: Know that salads are a very important balance to meals. It's a mellow bled to give you an edge to your pallet, it brings you a creaminess or a fresh earthy taste depending on the type of salad your enjoying with your meal. Serving your egg salad on crispy lettuce is a great combination – a one two knockout.

ALOHA COOKING

Paul Freeman

ALOHA COOKING
Paul Freeman

SOUPS OF THE DAY.

PORTUEGUES BEAN SOUP

ALOHA COOKING
Paul Freeman

Ingredients

1 large sweet onion dice
1 large carrot slice
1 tablespoon neutral Olive oil
3 stock celery medium diced
2 tablespoon tabasco sauce
1 tablespoon dark brown sugar
15 oz. tomato sauce
14 oz. can dice tomatoes
15 oz. can kidney beans undrain
4 cloves garlic crushed and peeled
2 pounds smoked ham hocks 3 Hocks 1 pound Portuguese sausage
1 large baking potato peeled and cut into 1 inch cubes
½ large head green cabbage chopped in thick pieces
1 teaspoon kosher salt add more to taste if needed
1 teaspoon ground black pepper add more if needed

Instructions

Step 1: Put ham hocks in large Dutch oven with 3 quarts water to cover meat. Bring to a boil then simmer with lid slightly open. Cook meat until starts to fall apart, 2-3 hours. Remove meat, let cool. Put broth in a large cooking pot measure broth at 2 quarts add more broth if needed. Pull meat off bone and set aside.

Step 2: Wipe clean Dutch oven, add oil heat to medium high add the sausage brown on all sides for 5 min. Reduce to medium low, stir in onion, celery, garlic carrots cook until onion is translucent about 10 mins.

Step 3: Add the 2 quarts reserved broth with potatoes, tomato's sauce diced tomatoes, kidney beans with liquid, sugar, black pepper, salt tabasco sauce give it a good stir increase heat bring it to a boil then reduce heat to a simmer. Cover let cook for 1 hour.

Step 4: Stir in cabbage letting it cook to a nice tender yet a firmness to it about 6-8 mins. Remove from heat let soup stand. Place a few ladles of this soup in a soup bowl on white rice or just as is, with some saltine crackers.

This here is a very welcoming soup whether under the weather or just needing a healthy bowl of a hearty soup to warm up that belly of yours. I for one enjoy this hearty soup. It has so much going on from the tasty chunks of the smoky flavor that the Portuguese sausage and ham hock brings, the flavory bright tomatoes, its sweet onion and the sweetness of the brown sugar complementing each other in this delicious soup.

BEEF SHANK SOUP

Ingredients

4 pound beef shank cut into 1½ cubes
1 tablespoon mince fresh ginger with 11/2 inch piece ginger thinly slice
3 quarts beef stock or water
1/3 cup dry sherry or ¼ whiskey
2 tablespoon neutral oil
5 whole star anise
6 dried Chinese red chili
zest from 1 small lemon
1 tablespoon light brown sugar
1-1/2 teaspoon fish sauce
6 oz. bok choy or mustard green cut crosswise into 3 inches
1 bunch cilantro chop for garnish

Instructions

Step 1: Pat dry meats, season with salt, ground black pepper and mince ginger let sit for 1 hour in fridge.

Step 2: At room temperature while waiting place dried shitake mushrooms in large bowl add 1-1/2 cup hot water 8-10 min. then save soaking water. Take mushrooms, cut bottom of stem and discard stem. Chop up the rest of mushrooms into slices.

Step 3: In large heavy pot heat oil on high heat till shimmering hot add beef shanks and ginger searing beef to brown on all sides 3-4 mins each side. Then deglaze pot with wine or whiskey, scraping up all its brown bits.

ALOHA COOKING
Paul Freeman

Step 4: When wine reduces then add beef stock and the reserved mushroom soaking liquids, mushrooms, star anise, chilies peanuts and lemon zest. Bring to a boil, then reduce to a simmer. Cook until meat is and tender 2 to 2-1/2 hours.
Step 5: Then add bok choy and cook 6 mins until tender with fish sauce. Let soup stand for 15-20 mins then serve with crackers and a little cheese.

PORK WATERCRESS SOUP

<u>Ingredient</u>

1 tablespoon vegetable oil   salt and pepper to taste
4 garlic cloves   2 tablespoon soy sauce
½ sweet round inion ¼ inch slices
1 can chicken or beef broth
1 bunch watercress chopped in 1/3
1 pound shoulder pork with little fat and cut thin slices

<u>Instructions</u>

Step 1: Heat pot on medium high with vegetable oil, add dice garlic, onion, and then pork strips browning it and caramelizing onion.
Step 2: Add soy sauce, kosher salt, and pepper to taste. Pour in broth and bring to a slight boil for 20 mins.
Step 3: Then put in the watercress for 5 mins. Cut stove off let soup stand for 5 mins then serve with rice or as is.
NOTES: These are just a few combinations of brothy or meaty soups that someone can make as is or add to it as desired.

ALOHA COOKING
Paul Freeman

DIPS AND SAUCES

CHEESY LOBSTER DIP

It's not difficult to make this cheesy lobster dip. This pleasurable hot dip will impress your guests. They'll come to love this hot cheesy lobster dip.

<u>Ingredients</u>
2 cloves of minced garlic
1 teaspoon of olive oil
¼ cup of chopped shallots
½ cup of sour cream
1 teaspoon mustard
kosher salt
Ground pepper
1 teaspoon of smoked paprika
6-8 oz. cooked lobster meat
8 oz. grated cheddar cheese
8 oz. softened cream cheese
2 tablespoons of grated Romano cheese
1/3 cup chopped fresh parsley

<u>Instructions</u>
Step 1: Pre-heat oven to 375 degrees.
Step 2: Heat skillet on med-high heat and add olive oil, shallots, and garlic. Sautee 1-2 minutes until fragrant and add salt and pepper
Step 3 – In a large mixing bowl, add the lobster meat, shallot/garlic mixture from the skillet, half of the cheddar

cheese, cream cheese, sour cream, Romano cheese, mustard, and paprika. Mix thoroughly.

Step 4: Add mixture to a safe baking dish spreading mixture evenly then adding the remaining cheddar cheese.

Step 5: Place baking pan in the oven and bake until cheese is golden and bubbly. Remove from oven and garnish with fresh parsley.

Take pan out and let it rest for 10 minutes. Use caution while serving as contents will still be fairly hot.

HAWAIIAN AVOCADO DIP

Ingredients

½ fresh lime juiced
½ cup diced onions
1 teaspoon Kosher salt
2 diced plum tomatoes
2 teaspoons of minced garlic
1 pinch of cinnamon (optional)
1 pinch of brown cayenne pepper
3 ripe avocados pitted and mashed
4 tablespoons fresh chopped cilantro
1/4 cup pineapple juice or ¼ cup of pureed pineapples

Instructions

Step 1: In a large bowl add in avocados smashing and mixing in lime juice, pineapples and salt.
Step 2: Fold in onions, cilantro, tomatoes, and garlic. Stir in cayenne pepper and cinnamon and fold thoroughly.
Step 3: Cover and refrigerate or serve immediately
NOTES: Serving immediately is the best way to go with this the fresher the better and with this being a dip having it at room tempture that it's at why not just enjoy it right there and then.

BAKE CRAB DIP

Ingredients

1 garlic clove minced
1 cup mayonnaise
1 cup soften cream cheese
1 tablespoon lemon juice
1 scallion thinly slice
1/3 cup swiss cheese
Couple crack of black ground pepper.
1/3 cup Yellow and Red bell pepper
1 teaspoon ground black pepper
1 tablespoon hot sauce(tobacco)

1 tablespoon cayenne pepper
½ small onion diced
1 tablespoon mustard
3 cups lumpy crab meat

Instructions

Step 1: Heat neutral oil in skillet on low heat adding in yellow plus red bell peppers and minced garlic sauté them just to open their flavors, then remove from heat and let cool.

Step 2: In large bowl mix together mayonnaise, cream cheese, lemon juice, hot sauce, and onions.

Step 3: Mix in a small bowl mayo, lemon oil, soy sauce, and 2 teaspoons sesame oil

Step 2: In a small nonstick pan heat to medium, add the rest of the sesame seeds, sugar, and a pinch of kosher salt. Cook for 2-3 min be sure to constantly stir until sugar caramelize to the sesame seeds. Then remove from pan onto a plate let it cool after it cools crush it up sprinkle on top of dip and garnish with thinly sliced scallion.

Step 3: Serve with crackers and or fresh vegetables sticks.

ALOHA COOKING
Paul Freeman

SOY SAUCE WITH ROASTED SESAME

Ingredients

2 tablespoons soy sauce

1 cup mayo

1 ½ teaspoon lemon zest

2 teaspoons lemon olive oil

3 teaspoons toasted sesame oil

1 red chili pepper thinly sliced

2 teaspoons roasted sesame seed

½ teaspoon kosher salt

1 tablespoon sugar

1 teaspoon black pepper

Instructions

Step 1:In a bowl mix together sugar, lemon, olive oil, soy sauce, lemon zest and mayonnaise.

Step 2: Toast sesame seeds and add to the bowl of mixture.

SWEET AND SOUR SAUCE

Ingredients
1 cup of pineapple juice
¼ cup of rice vinegar
1/3 cup of ketchup
¼ cup of soy sauce
2 tablespoons corn starch

1 red chili pepper thinly sliced
3 tablespoons of brown sugar

Instructions
Step 1: Add to sauce pan pineapple juice, soy sauce, rice vinegar, brown sugar, ketchup, corn starch, and red pepper.
Step 2: Bring sauce to a boil, then add ¼ water to cornstarch making a slur pouring it into boil saucepan.
Step 3: Reduce heat to a simmer, whisk constantly until sauce thicken then remove from heat.
Step 4: Let dipping sauce cool completely before using it for dipping.

HAWAIIAIN DIPPING SAUCE

<u>Ingredients</u>

1/3 cup soy sauce

1/4 cup white vinegar

1 cup pineapple juice

1/3 cup pineapple diced

1 tablespoon honey

1 tablespoon garlic cloves minced

2 tablespoons brown sugar

1 red chili pepper thinly sliced

1/3 cup orange juice

1 teaspoon fresh ginger

2 tablespoons cornstarch

1 teaspoon mustard

<u>Instructions</u>

Step 1: Add to sauce pan pineapple juice, orange juice, sugar, garlic, soy sauce, ginger, muster, vinegar, pineapple dices, and chili pepper.

Step 2: Bring sauce to a boil, then add ¼ water to cornstarch making a slur pouring it into boil saucepan.

Step 3: Reduce heat to a simmer, whisk constantly until sauce thicken then remove from heat

Step 4: Let dipping sauce cool completely before using it for dipping.

BBQ HAWAIIAIN SAUCE

<u>Ingredients</u>

½ cup ketchup
½ cup brown sugar
1/3 cup pineapple juice
1/3 cup soy sauce
6 garlic cloves minced finely
1 inch piece ginger grated finely
2 tablespoons chili garlic sauce
1 teaspoon red chili finely diced

1 teaspoon rice vinegar
1 teaspoon black pepper
1 teaspoon dry thyme
3 tablespoons sesame oil

<u>Instructions</u>

Step 1: Add all ingredients in a sauce pan stir and mix well.
Step 2: Bring to a boil and stir constantly, lower to a simmer cook until sauce thickens and reduces by half.
Step 3: Remove from heat and let cool this sauce is good for brush on while grilling, or baking. You also can use it to apply on cooked meats. This sauce goes with grill chicken, pork and beef dishes.

MRS. CASSANDRA BROWN BUTTER GARLIC SAUCE

<u>Ingredients</u>
½ stick butter   2 cloves minced

<u>Instructions</u>
Step 1: Heat small frying pan on medium heat add butter to pan.
Step 2: Right before butter starts browning add in minced garlic, cook until butter browns.
Notes: This goes good on Mahi Mahi (fish) dishes, and any other seafood dishes.

ALOHA COOKING
Paul Freeman

BEEF MEALS

ISLAND STYLE BEEF STEW

Ingredients
2 tablespoon soy sauce
4 garlic cloves minced
3 bay leaves
1 (6 oz. Can) Tomato paste
1 teaspoon kosher salt
4 cup Beef broth
1 pound boneless short ribs cut into 1 ½ inch cubes
2 large carrots cut into 1 inch pieces
1 pound brisket cut into 1 ½ inch cubes
3 celery stalk cut into 1 inch pieces
2 tablespoons all-purpose flour
1 sweet onion roughly chopped
2 tablespoons neutral oil
2 large potatoes peeled cut 1 inch
½ medium yellow onion diced
1 teaspoon ground black pepper

Instructions
Step 1: Season meats with salt and pepper, then coat with the flour.

ALOHA COOKING
Paul Freeman

Step 2: In a large pot or Dutch oven heat oil on medium-high get it nice and hot. Add the meats to brown it on all sides, for about 7-8 mins.

Step 3: Add in garlic and yellow onion, reducing heat to low, cooking it until onion soften about 8 mins.

Step 4: Add in soy sauce and tomato paste, then stir in broth with bay leaves, celery, potatoes, onion and carrots, raising heat so its boiling then lower to a simmer allowing meat to get tender. Cook time about 1 hour to 1 hour 20 minutes. Take off stove and let stand 25-35 mins.

Step 5: Serve with rice or crackers, and or just as is. You can't go wrong either way.

There is a song on the island that I can relate this very meal to and I encourage you to look it up and see for yourself if it resonates with you in any type of way. The song's name is, "ISLAND STYLE". And that's how we do it my bra'da and Sista's. Not only do we cook to eat, but we drink and sing for the enjoyment of living in the moment, and I can only hope that you all take this to heart as you learn that kani kapi la is the way to go. Hand in hand cooking, drinking and sing is our mixture for a great ole time for yourself as well as your ohana.

ALOHA COOKING

Paul Freeman

SWEET SOY SAUCE STEAK

Ingredients

1 cup mirin

5 scallion diced

ground black pepper

½ cup brown sugar

5 cloves garlic diced

½cup brown rice

1 cup soy sauce

½ cup whiskey

3 pounds boneless chuck roast or steak of choice 1 inch thick pieces.

2 tablespoon apple cider vinegar

2 inch piece fresh ginger peeled, sliced

Instructions

Step 1: Dab the steak dry, add pepper to steak let sit for 40-50 mins at room tempture.

Step 2: Place brown rice in grinder, let grind to a fine ground. Then toast ground up brown rice for about 5 mins keep stirring making sure not to burn rice.

Step 3: Reduce heat to medium low and add mirin, whiskey bring it to a boil scrapping up all the burn bits from bottom of pan. Then add soy sauce, brown sugar, ginger, vinegar, garlic, and scallions simmer and thicken sauce about 12-15 mins. Then remove aromatics and throw the solids away or strain sauce through.

Step 4: Prepare grill, rub steak down with black pepper and place on indirect heat cover grill let cook 20-25 mins yet flip steak when insert thermometer into the thickest portion of steak registers 105*F. Then checking every 5mins or so.

Step 5: Now place steak on direct heat and brush on sauce made earlier for 30 sec to 1 min. Flip and repeat brushing sauce on steak until a very nice glaze and internal temperatures reaches 125*F. This is for medium rare or a bit longer for desired doneness.

Step 6: Remove steak let rest for 8-10 mins then slice steak in thick pieces and serve with more sauce if desired. And eat with any sides that you'll like.

NOTES: For whatever reason you might like to go out to dinner more than often where it be for a quick fast food or diner's meal. I'd just like to recommend that you think twice about doing so and reconsider. So that you can cook yourself a well-deserved meal that is going to be satisfying even more than the fast food joint you was just about to go to. Just food for thoughts....

NOTES: LOW AND SLOW.

I can remember back when my bra dah John would school me about cooking. Those were the days, just having fun Bar BQ'n down at the beach or at the house. The laugher shared and learning something different with cooking from family members will always stick with me all my life and I hope that you as well take from this book what I have learned about cooking.

So here's a little tip for you all.

You might already know that low and slow cooking is the best way to go and that's diffidently correct. So whenever you're in a rush or feel the need to get your cooking done quickly. Just reset your heart and focus on what matters the most. That's not only advice for your cooking, it's also for your wellbeing in life. Because everyone needs a time to unwind, relax and just enjoy the moments in life... And the love of cooking can bring you just that, if you allow it to. Cooking is a great stress reliever when you are enjoying the passion of cooking.

If you're a lover of gravy and rice, this is a meal I can see you enjoying. Its many-layered deliciousness is like no other experience that you will experience. LOCO MOCO is well known in the Hawaiian islands. There are so many ways you can have this meal. It's your choice. Yet here is how my ohana cooks it up. So from my ohana to your ohana. So enjoy this very "gravyful" dish that can and will satisfy ones crave for a tasty gravy treat.

LOCAL MOCO
<u>Ingredients</u>

ALOHA COOKING
Paul Freeman

3 pound ground beef. 80/20
5 tablespoon unsalted butter or neutral oil
1 large onion diced
½ cup all-purpose flour or 4 tablespoon cornstarch
6 cloves garlic minced
2 ½ cups beef broth
8 large eggs
kosher salt and black ground pepper
4 teaspoon soy sauce
4 teaspoon Worcestershire sauce
2 stalk scallions thinly sliced for garnish
1 pot cooked white rice
6-8 mushrooms, for those who like mushrooms or you can leave mushrooms out of dish

Instructions
Step1: Heat skillet on medium high with 4 Tablespoons unsalted butter add onion with pinch kosher salt cook and stir onion until its translucent and soften 4-6min. Remove onion and place in a bowl until later.
Step2: Heat skillet on medium heat and add minced garlic to skillet, then the ground beef. Stir occasionally browning the meat and breaking up the meat to your desired bite size. Add a pinch of kosher salt, 4-6 mins until beef is cooked through. Remove ¾ of the ground beef from skillet. put it in a pot and stir in half of the onion. Cover and keep warm.
Step 3: Add flour to the rest of the meat that's in skillet, stir it together. Once flour is fully absorbed add soy sauce and Worcestershire sauce then beef broth continuing to cook

until gravy thickens. Add in the other half of the onion to the gravy (And if using corn starch, mix it with 3 tablespoons of water) making a slurry then stir it into skillet after beef broth has come to a simmer cook until gravy thickens.

Step 4: Fry egg sunny side up or fry egg leaving the yolk oozingly yolky.

Step 5: Assemble by placing 1-½ to 2 cups cooked white rice on plate, Then adding the ground beef on top the rice, place 2 fried eggs on ground beef and pouring the rich brown gravy over your eggs. You may garnish with mushrooms and scallions.

Notes: If you desire mushrooms then be sure that you cook mushrooms at the same time of cooking onions and adding them just as you would with the onion or you can ladle gravy after every layer. Starting with the rice, then meat, and finally eggs, just be moderate with the gravy if your pouring gravy on every layer. Or just go crazy with it! Once again, it's yours so own it.

LOCAL-KALBI

<u>Ingredients</u>
2 cups sugar
1/3 cup toasted sesame oil

ALOHA COOKING
Paul Freeman

3-½ cups soy sauce
1 tablespoon sambal
2 cups brown sugar
12 cloves garlic, peeled and crushed
Plus the following sides of your desired choice.
6 pounds short ribs cut a cross by ½ inch wide
4-inch pieces fresh ginger sliced and crushed
12 scallion cut into quarters and crushed
2 tablespoon sesame seeds, plus 1 tablespoon roasted for garnishing

Instructions
Step 1: In a large bowl mix together the soy sauce, sambal, sesame oil, sugar, scallion, ginger, garlic, 2 tablespoons sesame seeds.
Step 2: Clean and pat dry the short ribs. Add marinade mixture and short ribs together into a large topper wear container or zip lock bag mix them well. Refrigerate for at least 2-3 days top. Then toss and turn marinade meat ever 10-12 hours.
Step 3: Remove short ribs from fridge 1 hour before cooking so meat can come up to room tempture.
Step 4: Preheat grill and prep grill by cleaning and oiling it down with thongs and an oiled rag or paper towel. Then take your marinade meat from container, letting excess marinade drip off and place meat directly on the grill. Be very careful of flare ups. Grill time 3-4 mins each side until cooked through nice and juicy. Then transfer meat to serving tray let rest for 5 mins and serve with desired sides.

ALOHA COOKING
Paul Freeman

This Korean dish of kalbi stays in my heart for so many reasons. First and foremost the fond memories that it brings. The countless times that my childhood friend's gramma would be cooking when I'd come over. The homely smell of seasonings with its mouthwatering aromas filling the air and the offering to eat that she would always extend to me. I can assure you that the offer was never turned down (Big Smile). So there I was at my friend's home, eating away with no cares in the world, just me and the tasty kalbi. And if you would like the fullness of the bottom of the plate, try local style kalbi. Just plate it up with a scope or two of white rice, a scope of Kim Chee/di Kong, macaroni salad, shaved cabbage and fresh bean sprouts quickly blanched. You can't lose with this combination. Enjoy!

CHICKEN

HULI HULI CHICKEN

Ingredients

3 cups chicken stock

1/3 cup light brown sugar

1 tablespoon corn starch

garlic salt and oil.

ALOHA COOKING
Paul Freeman

1 stick unsalted butter
5 cloves garlic minced
2 tablespoon oyster sauce
1/3 cup pine apple juice

10 scallions roughly chopped
3 oz. ginger sliced and crushed

2 half parts of a whole chicken 1.1/2 -2 pounds for each half of whole chicken butterflied
2 tablespoon toasted sesame oil

Instructions
Step 1: Place chicken on sheet pan and rub shoi koji all over chicken. Cover with parchment paper and refrigerate overnight.
Step 2: Combined in medium sauce pan pineapple juice, chicken stock, brown sugar, oyster sauce, butter garlic, ginger, sesame oil, and scallions. Bring this to a boil then bring it to a simmer, let it simmer for 25-30 mins or until liquids reduce by half. Then remove any solids from sauce pan. Make a slurry with corn starch by adding 2 tablespoons of water and mixing it, pour slurry into sauce pan while stirring it bring it back to a boil. Then cut off heat.
Step 3: Take chicken out of fridge one hour before cooking it, allow chicken to come to room temperature. Rinse off the shoi koji from chicken then pat dry and season chicken with garlic salt.
Step 4: Heat grill on medium hot, prep grates with oil. If using coals to grill make two cook zones direct and indirect heat, or for gas, one side high and the other side low.
Step 5: Place each ½ chicken breast-side up, on indirect heat cover grill let cook for 8-10 mins, then start brushing

sauce onto chicken cover and let cook for another 8-10 mins. Then glaze chicken second time and flip chicken breast-side down on the direct heat and let chicken cook until skin begins to char lightly about 10 mins then glaze once again and flip chicken still on direct heat.

Hulu means to turn, so we are turning the chicken, and turning the chicken we are. Hulu Hulu chicken is a very meaningful cuisine that we Islanders truly take to heart. It's big part of my upbringing – was and still is. As you'll come to know that the Hulu Hulu chicken and its uniqueness, not just in taste butt also in the way that it supports our communities in so many ways. The countless fund raising we have with Hulu Hulu chicken sales are our way to not just feed bellies, it's a way to share the aloha that we have for each other. I would like to share that same Aloha with you all, so enjoy this cuisine of Hulu Hulu chicken. And know that Hulu is more than just a turn, it's a way of life and how we turn or the turns we take in life.

MRS CURRYS, CURRY CHICKEN.

This one goes out to you Ma. Much Aloha to you and the rest of the Ohana. We know you're looking down on us as we continue our Ohana ways of cooking and sharing of ourselves with others. As you can tell Mrs. Curry's Curry chicken really means a lot to me. Yes, I'm a mama's boy and I hope that this savory dish that my ma 'da taught me how to cook at a young age can be a part of your home as well.

ALOHA COOKING
Paul Freeman

So let's get this show on the road or better yet on the stove....

Ingredients

½ small yellow onion diced

3 bay leaves

3 cloves garlic minced

4 cup chicken broth

1 tablespoon mustard

1 ½-2 tablespoon yellow curry powder

2 large carrots cut into 1 inch pieces

1 ½ teaspoon kosher salt

2 large potato's cut into 1 ½ inch pieces

1 teaspoon crack of ground black pepper

2 celery stalk cut into 1/2 inch pieces

½ cup sweet onion roughly chopped

1/3 cup peanuts

½ teaspoon cinnamon

1/3 cup dry sherry

2 -2 ½ pounds chicken parts

Instructions

Step 1: Season chicken with salt and pepper, then coat with flour.

Step 2: Heat large pot or Dutch with oil on medium high. Get it nice and hot, then add pieces of chicken skin side down to pot. Browning it on each side for 3-4 minutes roughly 8 mins in all.

Step 3: Lower heat to low add garlic, curry powder, peanuts, mustard, soy sauce, and deglaze bottom of pot with dry sherry and broth. Then add bay leaves, potatoes, celery, carrots, and chicken bring it to a boil. Bring it back down to a simmer, cover pot, and let it stew for 1 hour to 1 hour 20 mins or until stew thickens.

Step 4: Remove from heat season to taste let it stand 20 mins, then serve with rice, crackers or just as is.

Well you all, now that you've try this meal of Mrs. Curry's Curry Chicken. How was your experience and what are any of your question about it? Not that I'll be able to know what your questions may be. Yet I just want you to know that you can make this meal your own by twisting it to your liking. You might not like peanuts or extra cinnamon. Please feel free to make it your own as I said before. Always remember that its s what you desire in your cooking not what others want. As my mom would say to me, "Boy it's what you want that matters, not what others want." So if you like it hot and spicy, add you some chili pepper water and or some straight hot chilis, a dash of this or a sprinkle of that....

ARARE FRIED CHICKEN
Ingredients
2 tablespoon chili paste

1-1/2 cup mochiko

3 large eggs

2 pinch kosher salt

3 tablespoon sugar

3 tablespoon mince fresh ginger

1 ½ tablespoon brown sugar

3 pounds boneless, skin chicken thighs

1 ½ cup all-purpose flour

3 tablespoon soy sauce

1 tablespoon sugar

3 tablespoon whisky

3 teaspoon garlic salt

ALOHA COOKING
Paul Freeman

½ cup plus 1 cup cornstarch

Instruction
s

Step 1: Mix in a large bowl ½ cup of the cornstarch, sugars, mochiko, and nice pinch of kosher salt. In a small bowl mix together the eggs, soy sauce, ginger, whiskey, chili paste, and 3 tablespoon water. Mix this into the large bowl of dry ingredients, be sure to mix thoroughly. Add chicken to bowl and mix by hand very well. Let it marinade for 6 hours or overnight.

Step 2: Remove marinade chicken from fridge, fill a large deep skillet or large bottom pot with 2 to 2-1/2 inches neutral oil. Be sure to have a few inches of clearance at the top of skillet or pot. Heat oil on medium high, try to maintaining 350*F throughout the frying process.

Step 3: Mix together the rest of flour, cornstarch, and garlic salt. Start by taking marinade chicken out of the bowl letting all excess marinade drip off. Then coat them very thoroughly in flour mixture, be sure to coat all wet spots. Place floured chicken on a large plate.

Step 4: Start frying battered chickens in batches, not overcrowding skillet or pot. Fry them to a nice golden brown about 5-6 mins. Turn chicken half way through. When done place them on an aired wire rack to cool.

Step 5: Assemble plate by first portioning the desired amount of cooked white rice, then place chicken on rice, sprinkle the furaki, aramixturere rice cracker on top, then garnish with thinly sliced scallions.

Have you ever heard of a Delicatessen? Well as kid growing up and going on school fieldtrips, there were times I was treated by my mom with a packed plate lunch bought at a local delicatessen. They served all kinds of cooked foods like fried noodles, fried rice, sushi, Teriyaki beef and chicken, egg rolls, chicken cut sue, Mana Pua, fried spam, egg fu yung, pork hash, and so much more. Yet this arare fried chicken always stuck out to me. Its sweet and crunchy meatiness, with a taste of seaweed mixed in. Man what I would give at this very moment to just have a bite of this arare fried chicken. I guess you'll just have to go fry me up some. L.O.L.

TERIYAKI GRILL CHICKEN

Ingredients

1/3 cup sake/dry sherry

6 scallion chopped

5 garlic cloves minced

1 1/2 cup sugar

1/3 cup brown sugar

3 inch piece ginger

2 cup soy sauce

3 pound chicken thighs skin on boneless.

Instructions

Step 1: Mix together in a large bowl soy sauce, sugar, brown sugar, scallions white, ginger and sake. Take 1 cup of marinade from bowl and place the boneless chicken breast into marinade mix it well cover it and put it refrigerator for 4-5 hours or for overnight.

Step 2: In a sauce pan bring the cup of marinade to a boil, then reduce to a simmer and let sauce thicken.

Step 3: 1 hour before cooking chicken remove it from fridge and let it come to room temperature.

Step 4: Prepare grill for indirect high heat. When grill is nice and hot, place marinade chicken with skin-side down on direct heat grill for 2-3 mins, then move chicken over to the indirect side of grill, still with skin-side down. Basting with reserved sauce and turning it often until it cooks through and thermometer reads 160*F at the thickest part of thigh. Set chicken aside for 2 mins. before serving with rice or eat just as is.

You may or may not had teriyaki grilled chicken, yet what's there to say then domo arrogato. Meaning 'thank you' to our bra da and sista of japan that shared this tasty meal which its sauce can go on all types of meats and poultry. I remember when I was nine years old selling newspapers on the street corner making money and at the end of my work day I'd buy myself a teriyaki meal at this one BAR BQ Diner. It's wonderful joys that it brought me will always be a part of my, "Love of Cooking." So take it from me or that young nine-year-old boy, what this Teriyaki Dish and its unique flavor can captivate your taste. And now I bid you a Sianara, meaning 'GOODBYE'.

PORK

KA'LUA PIG

Ingredients

6-8 pounds pork butt
2 ½ tablespoon kosher salt
½ cup soy sauce
foil to cook with
4 tablespoon liquid smoke
kosher salt
1/3 cup water
3 garlic minced

Ti leaves or banana or corn husk enough to wrap roast in thick layers

Instructions

Step 1: Make light incision to the pork roast. Season with salt all over, rub with the mixture of soy sauce and smoke liquid. Remove fibrous backbone of Ti leaves and wrap roast in leaves securing it with cooking string then in with foil.

Step 2: Place on a rack in shallow roasting pan and bake in a 500*F oven for 20-30 mins. Lower heat to 400*F and roast for 4-4 ½ hours. Remove foil, string and Ti leaves, discarding them. Let pork roast rest then tear apart roast adding 1 cup water and season with salt to taste.

Step 3: The rind can be removed from the pork roast. Place on a rack and cooked during the resting of the pork roast. Cook for 25-35 mins at 450*F or to nice a and crisp.

Step 4: 2 Tablespoons soy sauce combine with 1 Tablespoon fresh ginger finely diced 1/4 cup bourbon, and mix together and rub pork roast. This is a choice that you can do if that's something that interests you.

Step 5: Cooked up cabbage seasoned with soy sauce, garlic salt, ground black pepper, salt and garlic powder. This is just an option.

Now there are many traditional ways of cooking this kalua pig meal. We would normally roast the whole pig in the ground. In an Imu which is a "in the ground cook pit". That is the best way to go when cooking this meal. Yet that is for a bigger scale cooking such as a whole or half a hog. You also can have this with or without some cooked cabbage. I prefer with steamed/cooked cabbage to go with my Kalua pig. That's for you to decide for yourself, with or without cabbage. Drizzle a little Aloha soy sauce for an extra kick to your Kalua pig and you're on your way to a loving day.

PORK GUISANTES

<u>Ingredients</u>

½ yellow onion sliced
1 teaspoon kosher salt
4 cloves garlic minced
4 bay leaves
3 tablespoon tomato paste
¼ cup soy sauce
1 teaspoon ground black pepper
2 cups frozen green peas thawed
3 tablespoon apple cider vinegar
4 tablespoon condense cream of mushroom
2 pounds pork shoulder,/pork butt cut into 1 ½ inch thick and 1 inch thin

4 tabs unsalted butter
1/2 teaspoon ground cinnamon
2 tablespoon neutral oil
1 cup water

<u>Instructions</u>

Step 1: Mix in a large bowl the pork with salt, pepper, soy sauce, bay leaves and vinegar mix well cover refridge for 1 hour or overnight.

ALOHA COOKING
Paul Freeman

Step 2: In a large pot heat oil on high, when oil is nice and hot add garlic and onion and half marinade sauce cook for 2 mins. Then add the pork with the rest of the marinade. Stir and sauté for about 4 mins. Add 1 cup water and when it comes to a boil, reduce heat to low at a simmer, cover and let cook until pork is tender and cooked through, 25-35 mins.

Step3: Add the tomato paste and cream of mushroom, let cook for 2-3 mins, stir in the green peas let cook for 2-3 mins till peas gets bright green and tenders, add the 4 bats of butter with cinnamon, take off heat add salt and pepper to taste if needed. You may serve with rice or just as is.

I like to say that this Pilipino dish is a tasty meal that my gramma rose would put her foot into it. It might seem like a simple meal, but the fond emotions that flow through me make me want to share with you all, this dish which is more than just a meal, it's a comforting food that to this very day touches my heart. And as a ten-year-old kid going over to gramma's house for the weekend there's been so many times that I'd be right there with her in the kitchen cooking for the ohana. I learned many lessons about life during those times with my grandmother. Priceless moments like those are what I encourage you all to do with your ohana. You might just inspire that very someone in your life to become a person such as myself who loves cooking. I hope that I am shining that aloha on your love of cooking with this book of "Aloha Cooking".

PORK CHOP WITH BROCCOLINI AND MULTI-

COLOR BABY CARROTS

Ingredients

4 tablespoons honey

4 cloves garlic

 1 small sweet onion diced

4-5 tabs of butter

1 bunch broccolini

4 green apple peeled and diced

2 small thyme stems

olive oil

2/3 cup of apple cider

4 , ¾ inch thick pork chops

Instructions

Step 1: Take a large sheet pan, chop bundle of broccolini in half and cut baby carrots lengthwise, spread evenly on sheet pan with garlic cloves and generously drizzle olive oil over vegetables.

Step 2: Preheat large iron skillet with 2 Tablespoon oil on medium high heat.

Step 3: Pat pork chops dry and season them with salt and pepper, and place them in skillet. cook for 2 mins on each side. Them place skillet into oven with the sheet pan of

vegetables. With the oven set at 350*F, cook for 7-9 mins. Take pork chops out of skillet and let rest for 10 mins.
Step 4: Place skillet on medium high heat add the diced apples to skillet to cook the rawness out, add diced onion and finely diced thyme. Deglaze skillet with 1/3 apple cider, then add 4 tablespoons honey. Let sauce thicken, add the 4-5 tabs of unsalted butter at the end giving your sauce a nice creaminess.
Step 5: Place vegetables on a plate then the rested pork chop on top of vegetables and top it off with the sauce, aside of rice it's your choice or mash potatoes.

Ask yourself, is this something that you can see yourself cooking for a candlelight dinner for you and your significant other? I'm pretty sure that he or she would be very greatful. This meal, with a little wine, is a promising good time for you couples out there. I can't see you being in the dog house for it. So go for it, big dogs, you won't regret it. You only live once so you might as well treat them right.

SWEET AND SOUR SPARRIB "THE PINEAPPLE EXPRESS"

Ingredients

1 cup soy sauce

3 bay leaves

 1/3 cup oyster sauce

5 star anise

½ cup rice vinegar

2 cups dark brown sugar

1 tablespoon ground black pepper

1 (6 oz.) can pineapple juice

5 garlic peeled and crushed

1 (20 oz.) can reserve the juice

1 lemon cut in wedges to garnish

5 pounds pork spareribs cut into 2 inch pieces

3 tablespoon cornstarch

1 ½ cup apple cider vinegar

1 tablespoon kosher salt

Instructions

Step 1: Place spareribs in large pot with water covering it, bring to a boil, then to a simmer for about 4-5 mins, strain off water very well set aside to cool.

Step 2: Mix in a medium bowl the brown sugar, rice vinegar, cider vinegar, pineapple juice with the reserved juice from pineapple chunks, bay leaves, soy sauce, and star anise. Mix it very well.

Step 3: Coat cooled spareribs with cornstarch, salt and pepper, thoroughly.

Step 4: In a large pot or Dutch oven, heat up about 1 inch of neutral oil on high heat, getting it real hot. Place in batches so not to over crowd pot, browning spareribs all over 6-8 mins for each batch. Once spareribs are all done, drain the oil out of the pot.

Step 5: Put 1 tablespoon of oil back into the pot and heat on medium high heat, then add in garlic, ginger allowing it to open its fragrant, adding in the sauce mixture and spareribs, stirring it, coating the meat, then add water just up to spareribs, bring it to a boil, then lower heat to a simmer and adding then stirring in pineapple chunks. Cover with a lid and let cook until meat gets nice and tender about 1 hour cook time.

Step 6: Increase the heat to high and add in the oyster sauce, stirring it often continue cooking down the sauce to about half about 10-15 mins. Plate with some cooked rice and garnish with a lemon wedge plus any other sides of your choice.

This finger licking good meal will have your taste buds dancing to tunes that hits the highest of notes. Right through the rooftops and beyond the stars in the midnight sky. I can only hope that you enjoy this sweet savory dish as much as I do. I know that it's somewhat time consuming, but it's well worth the wait. Then again, the sour part of this dish just might not be what you're looking for in your meal. So cross out the garnish of lemon wedge and you'll be alright.

FISH

GRILLED FISH WITH GREENS AND COCONUT SAUCE

Ingredients

2 tablespoon neutral oil

1/3 cup sugar

1 whole fish 1 ½-2 pound

3 garlic minced

1 ½ inch piece ginger peel, thinly slice then into slivers

1 fresh red chili finely chopped

1 bunch spinach stems on washed

1 tablespoon arrowroot mix with 1 tablespoon water

1 (6 oz.)can coconut milk

1 lemon cut into 4 wedges

1 small onion

Instructions

Step 1: Heat oil in sauce pan on medium, adding half of the ginger to pan, frying it to a crisp. Remove from sauce pan to a paper towel and reserve the oil. With the other half of ginger, mix it together with garlic.

Step 2: Cut slits down the sides of fish and if its fillets cut slits on each side. Then rub fish with half of the garlic and ginger mix in between cut slits as well.

Step 3: Heat reserved oil in a skillet and add onion to skillet cooking about 5 mins. Then add remaining garlic and ginger mix along with red chili pepper for another 1 minute or so.

Step 4: Drain water off coconut milk and add milk with sugar to skillet bring to a boil then to a simmer for about 8-10 mins. Add in arrowroot slurry to thicken sauce and season with salt.

Step 5: Grill prepped fish for about 6-8 mins depending on size of fish or if its fillets.

Step 6: Blanch spinach in seasoned water of salt for 2-3 mins. Drain water off very well.

Step 7: Plate by layering first with spinach, then grilled fish, topped with the coconut sauce, garnish with fried ginger and squeeze lemon wedges.

Notes: Cook taro and cut into 1 ½ inch pieces then plate on the side of grilled fish and top with coconut sauce.

This is a cross dish of Laulau and Palusami. I would like to go more into dept with its contents, as well as why I left out other ingredients like taro, a staple of Hawaii's foods. For starters, this is just a quick version of the traditional style of this meal. And the real tedious details of fully prepping this dish will be a part of the second edition of ALOHA COOKING. I just wanted you to get little familiar with what's ahead to come. So until then which won't be long enjoy this delightful dish of Aloha.

INSIDE OUT STUFF AHI

Ingredients

ALOHA COOKING
Paul Freeman

4 nice size AHI, steak 'tuna'
1-1/2 pound emotion crab meat lumps or shredded
ground black pepper
kosher salt
1-½ cup mayonnaise
1/3 cup onion diced
1/3 cup scallions
1/3 cup celery thinly sliced Julian cut
½ cup mozzarella cheese grated
1/3 carrots thinly sliced Julián cut
1 teaspoon paprika
2 tablespoon neutral oil

Instructions
Step 1: In a large bowl mix together ½ of scallion, celery, carrots, imitation crab meat, 1 cup mayonnaise, grated mozzarella and onion fold in this mixture well, and if needed add more mayonnaise to crab stuffing. We are looking for a nice thick mixture, not runny.
Step 2: Pat dry fish steaks, season them with salt and pepper. Add them to a large skillet hot of oil on medium high heat. Sear the fish steaks on both sides about 1 ½ -2 mins keeping the middle of fish pink we are not cooking them right now.
Step 3: Place fish steaks on a baking sheet pan and cover them all over and around fish steaks, with the crab stuffing mixture.
Step 4: Place baking sheet on middle rack in preheated oven at 350*F, bake for 12- 15 mins, then under the broiler for 4- 5 min. Bake until fish cooks and stuffing crust crisp

up. Remove from oven and let set about 2- 3 minutes.
Garnish with the rest of scallions and paprika. Then serve
with a side of salad.

Sorry my Bra Dah John I might have butchered your Stuff
Ahi, Nah, I followed your step by step recipe like you told
me. Yes people from time to time I will have a family, friend
or that someone special enough to drop me a recipe to
hand down for you all. It's not that I can't go without doing
so. This is just how we islanders are sharing, caring, and
loving. So go for it and make yourself an Inside Out Stuff
Ahi.

CHARRED FISH

Ingredients

1 whole fish, 3 pound, scaled and cleaned
3 cloves garlic peeled and crushed
3 tablespoon tamarind concentrate
½ onion sliced
1-1/2 tablespoon fish sauce
4 scallions thinly diced
2 bay leaves
1 cup cherry tomato cut in half
1-1/2 inch piece fresh ginger thinly sliced
1/3 cup sweet pineapples chunks
1 red chili pepper diced
2 tablespoons cilantro thinly chopped

Instructions

Step 1: Heat grill to hot, prep grill grate with oil. Brush fish with oil and start to grill, Be sure to let fish get a good char before turning fish over, turn fish and cook fish through it's okay if fish is burned in places cook time about 16-20 mins. Remove from grill and place on sheet pan let cool then use a fork to remove charred skin, fillet fish from bone and cut the fish's head off.

ALOHA COOKING
Paul Freeman

Step 2: Place charred skin, fish bones and fish head into a soup pot, add 4 cups of water with bay leaves, 1 inch piece fresh ginger, and crushed garlic cloves. Bring to a boil, then lower heat and simmer for 30 mins. Then strain broth and discard solids return broth to soup pot and add in dashi powder, tomato, fish sauce, onion, tamarind concentrate, chili pepper, and ginger. Let it simmer for about 10 mins or until the onions turn translucent.

Step 3: Plate charred fillets with rice, ladle soup in a bowl and garnish with fresh pineapple chunks and cilantro.

Notes: You can use just fish steaks, yet just watch your cook times when doing so.

Have this charred fish with a nice red wine, you can't go wrong. And for those that don't drink, it's still nice to have a glass of red wine with this charred fish, Nah! Just kidding, if you don't drink, it's alright that you have yourself a nice fresh fruit drink such as Passion orange, Grava juice, or any other desired fresh fruit drink you would like. It will give it a pop.

ESCABECHE

<u>Ingredients</u>
4 fish filets
2 tablespoon neutral oil
2 small green peppers
3 mince garlic
kosher salt
½ cup water
1 large onion chopped
3 tablespoon Apple cider vinegar
1 teaspoon ground black pepper
1 ½ tablespoon brown sugar
1 tablespoon cornstarch mixed in 2 tablespoon water
½ teaspoon finely chopped fresh ginger

<u>Instructions</u>
Step 1: Pat dry fish and season with salt.
Step 2: Heat oil in large skillet on medium high. Then add in the seasoned fish sauté them on both sides and let them set.
Step 3: Add the garlic, onions, to skillet cooking until onions are translucence, then add in water, green peppers, ginger, and brown sugar. Bring it to a boil and mix in cornstarch slur, lower heat to a simmer cook to sauce thickens, then add fish back in skillet cooking for 2-3 mins.

ALOHA COOKING
Paul Freeman

Step 4: Plate fish with sauce on rice and any sides of your choosing.

Just a little something for you all to enjoy. Not that it's a time saver to cook these meals. Yet I know there are times in our lives that when we are off to the races. There's nothing like just taking one for the road. I have to say that my love for cooking surly helps me with a lot of my life stress. Even though we as human beings carry the heavy loads of our life situations and there might be times that you're not able to have someone to hear you out. I strongly suggest that you turn to this book and cook yourself a little something-something. You can't go wrong with a nice meal or treat. You see food is a simulant that gets us in a happy and joyful mood. So go find yourself a happy place in this book. I'm sure you'll be able to find the one meal or treat that will put your day at ease.

RICES/PASTAS NOODLES

HAWAIIAIN STYLE FRIED RICE

<u>Ingredients</u>
1 (6 oz.) can spam
4 cups cook white rice
3 recess peanut butter cups
4 large eggs
1/3 cup pineapples diced
2 stalk scallions thinly slice
1 tablespoon garlic minced
2 tablespoon soy sauce
1 cup Portuguese sausage
ground black pepper
kosher salt 1 teaspoon white pepper
(Be sure that your pineapples are really sweet one's)

<u>Instructions</u>
Step 1: Heat oil in a large frying pan or Wok on medium high heat and fry up diced spam, giving it a nice crisp. Remove from pan and scramble the eggs, salt and pepper them, and remove from pan.

Step 2: Add minced garlic to frying pan, stir it and mix in rice, continue to stir every 30-40 sec. Add in soy sauce, green onion, salt and pepper to taste, mix in the spam and scrambled eggs continuing to stirring it.

Step 3: Plate fried rice and garnish with pineapple dices and place a Reese's peanut butter cup on the side of fried rice.

Step 4: Eat the peanut butter cup to open up your pallet for the fried rice.

Yes, I'm trying to tickle your funny bone. Although Spam and peanut butter cups does set well with a lot of Hawaii locals. This is just to open up your creativeness with your own cooking as well as to experience something new. You see the peanut butter cup will give you a creamy sweet and very light good bitter tart taste as you eat the fried rice. So go give it try, you might just find your new favorite fried rice.

GANDOLE RICE

<u>Ingredients</u>

3 cups uncooked white ice
4 cloves garlic finely minced
1 tablespoon Achiote oil
1/3 pound bacon
1 small onion diced
5 green onion thinly sliced
3 cups chicken broth
2 packets Sazon Goya
1 (8 oz.) can tomato sauce
1 (15 oz.) Gandule Verdes

ALOHA COOKING
Paul Freeman

1 teaspoon garlic salt
1 bunch cilantro finely chopped
½ large green bell pepper diced
1 (6 oz.) can pitted black olives
1/3 pound pork tenderloin sliced thinly in strips

Instructions

Step 1: Clean rice and set aside. In a large skillet, heat on medium high, add Achiote oil, bacon, garlic salt, and pork. Cook until meat browns about 8-10 minutes.

Step 2: Add to skillet garlic, bell pepper, and onion, cook until onions become translucent. Then adding green onion, and cilantro, stir well and heat through. Remove skillet from heat and set aside.

Step 3: Add to the rice that's in the rice cooker, chicken broth, tomato sauce, olives, Sazon Goya packet, and Gandule beans.

Step 4: Drain oil from cooked pork and reserve it. Then add pork to rice cooker stirring it well combining everything and then start cooker.

Step 5: Once rice is done cooking, remove rice from rice cooker into large skillet fluffing it, adding 3-4 tablespoon of reserved pork grease.

Notes: If you don't have a large enough rice cooker, you can cook it on the stove top in a large cooking pot with a lid. Cook time about 35-45 minutes starting at medium high, then lower to medium, to medium low stirring it every now and then so that it don't burn on the bottom pot or skillet.

KIM CHEE FRIED RICE

<u>Ingredients</u>
Furikake seasoning
4 tabs unsalted butter
2 teaspoons sesame oil
1-1/2 tablespoon soy sauce
5 cups cooked rice
5 scallion thinly sliced
1 medium yellow onion
5 large eggs
1 teaspoon Korean chili paste
8 oz. bacon thick cut and chopped
kosher salt/ ground black pepper
2 cups Kim Chee drained well roughly chopped, reserve
3 tablespoons of Kim Chee juice

<u>Instructions</u>
Step 1: Heat a large non-stick skillet on medium high and cook bacon to a nice brown about 10 mins. Remove bacon and save bacon grease.
Step 2: Place same skillet on medium heat and add in 1 tablespoon of bacon grease. Add in onion cooking it for about 4 mins at this time stir in chili paste.
Step 3: Add in the rice, stirring in soy sauce, Kim Chee juice and 1 tablespoon bacon grease. Increase heat to high and evenly spread rice in skillet and cover it letting it cook until it browns, about 3-4 mins.
Step 4: Scrape and flip rice from the bottom of skillet and repeat browning for 2-3 mins then stir in Kim Chee, 1

tablespoon bacon grease, bacon, scallions and sesame oil.
Cook for about 2 mins seasoning with salt and pepper.
Place the fried rice in a large bowl and cover with foil.
Step 5: Crack all 4 eggs into a small bowl. Then wipe skillet
clean add 1 tablespoon bacon grease heat skillet on medium
high. When grease gets hot carefully add the 4 tabs of
butter to skillet. After butter melts, gently add in the eggs
and cover with a see through lid lower heat to medium let
cook for 1 min and remove skillet from stove.
Step 6: Place fried rice plates then add 1 fried on top of rice
garnish with the rest of scallions.

Well this fried rice is really for those that love Kim Chee. I
know that I can eat Kim Chee right out of the Kim Chee jar
and just eat the whole jar at that. Yet what says you? Can
you see yourself cooking this dish? All I can say is don't
knock it until you've tried it. Who knows, this might just be
your go-to side-dish for your next meal.

TAI LEMON RICE

<u>Ingredients</u>
2 oz. snow peas
¼ crushed red pepper
2 cups water
1 tables soy sauce
4 green onion sliced
1 tablespoon mince garlic
1/3 teaspoon ground ginger
2 cups cooked pork or chicken
¼ cup salted peanuts chopped
4 tablespoon fresh cilantro chopped
½ large lemon cut into 4 wedges
1 package 5-6 oz. lemon and jasmine rice pilaf, (Rice mix)

<u>Instructions</u>
Step 1: Heat a large skillet on medium high add water, soy
sauce, crushed red peppers, ginger, and mince garlic. Bring
it to a boil and add in rice mix, stirring it as you bring it
back to a boil again. Then lower heat to a simmer, cover it,
and let cook for about 12-15 mins.
Step 2: Add in your desired meats, snow peas, half cilantro,
and half green onion, stirring it in and letting it cook for
about 4-5 min or until meat is well heated and peas have
softened and turning a bright green.
Step 3: Plate rice on serving plates, garnish with the rest of
scallions and cilantro. Squeeze a lemon wedge over the rice.

PANCIT

Ingredients

1 pound fresh egg noodles, chow mein noodles (Pancit Conton)

6 oz. ground pork

kosher salt

¼ cup oyster sauce

1 teaspoon ground annatto

2 tablespoons minced garlic

1 medium carrot thinly slice

4 scallions cut into 1 inch pieces

½ medium red onion thinly sliced

5 oz. green cabbage copped in 2 inch pieces

8 oz. boneless, skinless chicken thighs chopped into 1 ½ inch pieces

16 peeled and deveined large shrimps

2 teaspoon instance dashi powder

1 medium tomato sliced into strips

1 cup chicken stock

1 tablespoon soy sauce

¼ cup fried garlic

Instructions

Step 1: Heat salt water in a large pot, bring it to a boil and add egg noodles to water just to blanch them. Cook them no more than 2 mins. Drain very well and add 1 tablespoon neutral oil and stir.

Step 2: Mix together in a small bowl the stock, soy sauce, oyster sauce, fish sauce, dashi powder, and annatto.

Step 3: Heat the 3 tablespoons neutral oil in a Wok or large skillet on high heat. Then add in garlic, chicken, pork, cook until meat is mostly done then add in shrimp stir fry until shrimps are slightly pink.

Step 4: Add the carrots and cook for 2-3 mins. Then stir in cabbage, onion, tomato, noodles, with stock mixture and stir fry until noodles are heated through and sauce is about gone.

Step 5: Garnish with scallions, and fried garlic. Toss them through plate then serve.

CHICKEN HEKA

Ingredients

1 small onion sliced
1 carrot sliced
8 oz. bamboo shoots
5 garlic cloves minced
2 inch piece ginger Julien slice
3 stalks scallions cut into 1 inch pieces
1 bunch watercress cut in half
1 pound boneless, skinless chicken thighs cut into 1-½ inch pieces.
1 cup about 8 shitake mushroom soaked (in hot 1 cup chicken broth)
5 oz. cellophane noodles (bean thread)

2 cups chicken broth
½ cup soy sauce
1 tablespoon sesame oil
1/3 cup mirin

Instructions

Step 1: In large skillet, brown the chicken over medium high. Heat for 2-3 mins add ginger and let the garlic sauté for 2-3 minutes more.

Step 2: Add the chicken broth, mirin, soy sauce, and sesame oil. Then bring to a boil.

Step 3: Add in onion, carrots, shitake mushrooms, and bamboo shoots, mix well and turn heat on low. Put lid on pot let simmer 5 minutes.

Step 4: Add the cellophane noodles. Cook for 6-8 mins, or until noodles are cooked through and most of the liquids have been absorbed. You don't want it soupy, just saucy.

Step 5: Add scallions and watercress stir through cook for 1-2 minutes. Serve as is or plate over some rice.

SHRIMP ALFREDO

Ingredients
1 pound shrimp (31-40 count size) thawed, peeled, deveined, tails optional.
4 oz. cream cheese soften cut into pieces
¾ cup heavy whipping cream
2 tablespoons butter
2 garlic cloves minced
¼ cup chicken broth
1 cup freshly grated parmesan cheese
kosher salt
1 teaspoon ground black pepper

Instructions
Step 1: Heat large pot of salted water to cook fettuccine pasta. Cook until dente.
Step 2: In a large skillet on medium heat add in butter, garlic cream cheese, cream, and broth. Stir as everything melts together, about 3-4 minutes.
Step 3: When cream cheese melt down, add in grated parmesan. Stir it into sauce about 1 minute.
Step 4: Add the pre-prepare shrimp to pan cook for about 5 minutes, stir occasionally.
Step 5: Season shrimp alfredo with salt and pepper to taste. Toss and garnish with diced pineapple. Serve and enjoy this Island style shrimp alfredo.
This one goes out to my favorite woman in my life. Knowing what she likes and how she likes it, creamy and

sweet, flavorful, with waves of enjoyment. So what do you say about this lavish seafood dish of deliciousness? No worries if this dish don't get your taste buds excited. There are always other dishes for you in this book for you. Aloha and like always, enjoy.

ALOHA COOKING
Paul Freeman

POKE

TRADITIONAL HAWAIIAIN STYLE POKE.

Ingredients

3 pound Ahi tuna shichimi grade cut into1/2 inch cubes
¾ cup diced onions,
1-1/2 tablespoon Hawaii sea salt or flake salt
4 tablespoon roasted finely chopped or ground Kukui nut
½ cup chopped Ogo seaweed fresh
3 Hawaii chili pepper or 2 birds eye peppers, thinly sliced
½ cup thinly sliced scallion

Instructions

Step 1: In large bowl, fold in gently the fresh tuna, onion, salt, chili, seaweed. Thoroughly mix. Then add nuts and scallions, fold in once again, seasoning if needed. Serve immediately or place in an air tight container and refrigerate. Re-salt if needed after refrigeration.
 Notes: You may add to this traditional style poke by, adding soy sauce, sesame oil, and garlic salt even a little chili pepper water. These added seasoning and sauces truly complement this dish. Well, enjoy this wonderful island dish, my friends. ALOHA.

FRIED POKE

Ingredients

crack of black pepper
2 teaspoon soy sauce
1 tablespoon sesame seed
2 cloves garlic minced

ALOHA COOKING
Paul Freeman

2 tablespoon sambal oelek
2 tablespoon scallion thinly slice
1 pound fresh or leftover poke

Instructions

Step 1: Heat a wok or skillet over high heat coat with oil. Add garlic and when oil starts to smoke, add poke. Be very careful at this point. Stir-fry for a few seconds just to sear fish's outsides, yet leaving the inside of fish still raw. Add sambal, sesame seed and soy sauce toss for a few more seconds. Remove from heat and plate fried poke top with chopped scallions and black pepper. Serve with rice or poi, or eat as is....

PARADISE POKE
Ingredients
1 roughly diced cucumber
1/3 med sweet onion diced

1/3 cup Ogo sea weed
½ cup Tamari dressing

5 cups 1 inch cubes of sturdy vegetables sweet potatoes, taro or both with radish, parsnip, yuca, and turnips
olive oil
kosher salt and ground black pepper
2 tablespoon roasted macadamia finely chopped

Instructions
Step 1: Mix the 5 cups of 1 inch sturdy vegetables in large bowl with olive oil, then place vegetables on a baking sheet. Bake for 16-20 mins, until tender yet firm. Take them out and let rest and cool about 10 mins.
Step 2: Then transfer and divide in 2 bowls, toss with Tamari dressing place half and half of cucumber, onion, radishes, sea weed gently fold in together with more dressing to taste.
Notes: You may add fresh poke right on top or just eat as is. This can be a vegetarian dish or you can make it your own if you desire to add raw fish to it.

COCONUT POKE
Ingredients
3 pounds Ahi tuna
2 tablespoon sugar
1/3 cup ogo sea weed chopped

1/3 cup sweet onion diced
1 ½ tablespoon flake salt

ALOHA COOKING

Paul Freeman

½ cup scallion finely chopped
2 Hawaii chili pepper thinly sliced
2 tablespoon kukui or macadamia nut crushed and chopped
4 tablespoon toasted sweet coconut shreds
1/3 cup coconut milk plus 2 tablespoons condense milk

Instructions

Step 1: Heat in sauce pan coconut milk, condense milk. Add in sugar on medium high heat, then lower heat to low. Continue to thicken sweet coconut sauce, then let sauce completely cool 30-40 mins.

Step 2: Cut Ahi Tuna into ½ inch pieces, then place in large bowl and fold in onion, scallion, macadamia nuts, Hawaii chili pepper and ogo sea weed. Season with salt flakes.

Step 3: Add your nicely cooled coconut sauce to large bowl, gently folding in with coconut shreds. Place into a serving bowl to be served best eaten right away.

Notes: Know that you can just garnish with sweet coconut shreds and leave out the coconut sauce, this is up to you. I prefer the coconut sauce as it brings a much richer flavor to your taste buds. Its sweet richness cuts through very well with other things that you'll be eating at the same time. Take it from me, a man with a sweet tooth and a joyful jolly belly.

ALOHA COOKING
Paul Freeman

ALOHA COOKING
Paul Freeman

DESSERTS

HAUPIA this savory tasteful extra rich and creamy coconut pudding like treat is an iconic Luau desert of Hawaii. This thick, and not too sweet, creamy treat has been made back in the old Hawaiian days by freshly milling coconut and thickening it with ground arrow root, then wrapping it up in Ti or banana leaves. Then it would be baked in an Imu, which is an underground oven. Its consistency is between a Jell-O pudding and a custard. And if you're a person that loves coconut, this here is going to be a wonderful delight for your taste buds.

HAUPIA

Ingredients

1 cup sugar
oil or butter to grease pan
1 teaspoon vanilla extract
1 14 oz. can full fat coconut milk
1/3 cup coconut flakes, toasted.
6 tablespoons arrowroot powder or 1/3 cup cornstarch

Instructions

ALOHA COOKING
Paul Freeman

Step 1: Start by mixing together the 6 tablespoon arrowroot or 1/3 cup cornstarch with ¾ cup of water until it's nice and smooth.

Step 2: In a saucepan combine the coconut milk, sugar, and vanilla extract. Bring it to a boil on medium-high heat. Add the mixture of arrowroot slowly into the saucepan, remember to constantly stir. Bring heat down to medium-low, continuing to stir for about 7 to 8 mins. Until it is pearlescent.

Step 3: Prepare an 8 by 8 pan, 4-6 inches in height, slightly grease pan with oil or butter then pour Haupia mix in pan. Let cool to room tempture, then refrigerate for a good 3 hours.

Serve this as is, or you can plate it with fresh diced fruits just don't over power your main part of dessert and be sure to use something to complement the richness of the haupia.

PANI POPO.

Ingredients

20. frozen dinner rolls depending there size or homemade rolls.

10 oz. can coconut milk

1.cup sugar

Instructions

Step 1: Coat a 9 by 13 baking pan with cooking spray. Arrange rolls evenly to thaw. If using homemade rolls, roll dough into golf size balls and arrange them the same way as frozen rolls.

Step 2: Allow rolls to rise double in size, 4-5 hrs.

Step 3: Preheat oven to 350*F.

Step4: In large bowl combine coconut milk and sugar mix until sugar dissolves.

Step 5: Pour 2/3 of the coconut mixture over the rolls, then place into oven for 25-30 minutes, or until dough is cooked through.

Step 6: Remove from oven and pour the remaining coconut mixture over the top evenly.

Step7: The rolls will be nice and sticky, It can be served hot or cold. Notes: BEST MADE WITH FRESH DINNER ROLLS. This special desert is from our pacific islands of Samoan which is rich in flavor that you can come to love. I would like to say that when writing this desert recipe for you all. I just couldn't help myself to think back to my younger days as a kid and going to the neighborhood grocery store bakery to buy this delightful desert treat. And the task there at that time was to get the money to buy a couple of PANI POPO. Whether it was picking mangos and selling them or cleaning someone's yard, I was going to get my PANI POPO!!!!!!

ALOHA COOKING
Paul Freeman

NESTLES CHEESECAKE

<u>Ingredients</u>

3 large Eggs
½ cup sour cream
kosher salt
3 tablespoons sugar
8 tablespoons plus (stick)
unsalted butter melted
16 oz. cream cheese at
room temperature

13.5 oz. sweetened
condenses milk
2 tablespoon fresh pine
apple juice
1-1/2 cup graham cracker
or any cookies , finely
crushed.

½ cup Nestle's Quick
powder of your flavor of
choice

Instructions

Step 1: Heat oven to 325*F and grease a Springform or a 9" pie pan with butter.

Step 2: Mix together the 1 1/2 cup finely crushed graham crackers with ½ cup Nestle's Quick powder, melted butter, and a pinch of salt. When mixture is nice and moist, place it into greased springform, press crust evenly to the bottom and up the side of pan. Bake the crust for 8-10 minutes, take out and let it rest till your done with the filling.

Step 3: Be sure that your cream cheese and sour cream is at room tempture when you mix them together in a mixer until fluffy, fold condensed milk, add eggs and pineapple juice, till you have a good consistency. Then pour into crust Springform.

Step 4: Place Springform back in oven for 50 min. to 1 hour finishing test. Take a tooth pick stick in the center of cheese cake and if it comes out clean, then it's done.

Step 5: Remove cheesecake let it rest, then refrigerate for 1-2 hours, garnish with a dash of Nestle's Quick and curd you might like.

HALO HALO

Ingredients

mango jelly-o

¼ cup mango nectar

2 ripe mangoes peel cut into bite size pieces

1 envelope unflavored powder gelatin about 2-1/2 teaspoon

FLAN
½ cup plus 2 tablespoons unsweetened coconut milk
¼ cup plus 2 tablespoon. Sugar
4 large egg yolks
½ teaspoon vanilla extract
¼ teaspoon kosher salt

CORN AND ASSEMBLY
3 tablespoon sugar
1 teaspoon diamond crystal or ½ teaspoon kosher salt
1 teaspoon vegetable oil
¼ cups small sago pearls
1 ½ cup unsweetened coconut milk
¼ cup sweetened shredded coconut
1 pint Ube ice cream or your choice of creamy flavored ice
cream
1 14oz can pondon or regular sweetened condensed milk
½ cup macapuno
1 cup sliced strawberry's
½ cup drain palm seeds, dyed green or of your choice
sweetened red beans and toasted pinipig

INSTRUCTIONS FOR MANGO JELLY-O
Step 1: Add into blender lime juice, lime zest, mango nectar,
1/3 mangoes, a pinch of kosher salt bled to very nice and
smooth texture.
Step 2: Heat gelatin and ½ cup water in a small sauce pan
over medium heat constantly stir until gelatin dissolves.
Remove from heat and stir in mango puree. Pour Jelly into
9x5 loaf pan and carefully fold in rest of mangoes. Wrap
tightly and let chill until it sets 25-30 mins.
This can be done 4-5 days ahead of time.
INSTRUCIONS FOR FLAN
Step 1: Preheat oven 350*F, place rack in middle of oven. Then
cook sugar and 1 tablespoon with water in sauce pan over
medium heat stir until sugar devolves. Swirl pan occasionally
until it reaches an amber color, roughly 8 mins. Scrape
caramel into another 9x5 loaf pan.
Step 2: Whisk egg yolk, coconut milk, condense milk, vanilla,
and salt in small mixing bowl. Pour through a fine-mesh sieve
into loaf pan of caramel. Cover, then set inside a roasting pan

and into oven. Carefully pour water in roasting pan about half way up to loaf pan.

Step 3: Bake flan until it set in the center. Cook to a barely golden top 50-60 mins. Let sit and cool then chill for 4 hours.

Step 5: Spread out corn on rimmed baking sheet, sprinkle sugar and kosher salt, then drizzle oil over it toss and roast until crisped slightly to a light golden brown 10-15 mins. Meanwhile bring sago pearls with ½ cup water to a simmer in small sauce pan cook until translucent with firm tenderness, 8-10 mins. Drain, then combine in small bowl with coconut milk, stir well to separate pearls, let set to cool. Toast coconut shreds in small skillet over medium heat until edges turn brown and crisp about 5 mins.

Step 6: Cut flan into bite size pieces, divide between four tall glasses, cut out mango jelly place on flan, add scoop of ice cream, condense milk, shaved ice, strawberry, macapuno palm seed, corn sago pearl, toasted coconuts, red beans and pinipig as desired.

ALOHA COOKING
Paul Freeman

MRS. OSWEILER BUTTERCOOKIE CHEESECAKE DELIGHT

<u>Ingredients</u>
<u>FOR CRUST</u>
¼ cup,(½ stick) melted butter plus more for pan
35 Bisscoff or Specalous cookies
1/8 teaspoon kosher salt

<u>FOR CHEESCAKE</u>
1 ¼ cup sugar
½ teaspoon kosher salt
4 large eggs beaten
¼ cup sour cream
3 cups heavy cream
½ cup cookie butter
1 teaspoon pure vanilla extract
32 oz. cream cheese softened
10-12 caramel candy melted

<u>FOR GARNISH</u>
6 caramel candy melted
6 Bisscoff or Specaloos cookies
1/3 Cup cookie butter melted

<u>Instructions</u>
Step 1: Grind up 36 cookies in grinder and place in large bowl and mix in melted butter with salt combine very well.
Step 2: Place pie crust mixture in Springform pan, then evenly press crust down and up the side of pan and let set.

Step 3: In a large mixing bowl add the softened cream cheese, sugar, salt, heavy cream, vanilla extract, cookie butter melted, and eggs. Then mix ingredients very well and add in melted caramel, giving it a stir.

Step 4: Pour cheesecake mixture into crust pan and water bath cheesecake by placing spring form into a deep baking pan with water 1/3 high up spring form so that the water doesn't bubble over into cheesecake. Be sure to check water level as you bake cheesecake.

Step 5: Preheat oven to 350*F and bake for 45-50 mins. Finishing test, take tooth pick stick in the center and if it comes out clean, then it's done. Remove from oven and let cool.

Step 6: Refrigerate cooled cheesecake for 2-3 hours. Remove and garnish with crushed up cookies, melted caramel candy, and melted cookie butter. Place back in refrigerator for 30 or until topping sets on cheesecake. Serve and enjoy.